Empathy

Empathy

Lauren Kirby

I'm afraid for people to see me
    I'm afraid they won't like what they see
So I always put my guard up
And tell myself there is no one I can trust
Even if it makes me lonely

{ 2 }

If I come off cold, I don't mean to
     I've just got some things I'm trying to work through
Please forgive me if I'm not playing nice
It's just my pain that makes my heart as cold as ice

My envy grows like ivy
Green and impossibly tangled
For those who don't feel what I feel
Skin unmarred, chest not painful

So if I come off cold, I don't mean to
I've just got some things I'm trying to work through
Please forgive me if I'm not being nice
It's just the feeling that every day will be as dark as night

{ **3** }

It's the fading of a smile
    As I round the corner
It's the excuse to leave the room
The moment I come in
And maybe it's all in my head
But I don't think it is
It's hard not to notice
When overthinking begins

{ **4** }

Tell me how it feels being up there in the castle
    Do you get despondent being up there all alone?
I imagine that the ghosts lurk in every corner
Their shadows only reminding you of the seeds that you have
sown

Is your fortune still magnificent
When no one is around to share it with?
Is your success still glorious
With no one around to honor it?

With every despotic decree
Your reign grew ever further
Without you even realizing
Isolation approaching with fervor

Tell me how it feels being up there in that castle
So far removed, above it all
Back straight, standing tall
Feigning indifference with steely resolve

Tell me how it feels looking down on happy people
Ruling with an iron fist
Tyranny at its finest
Even though your followers aren't faithful

As the day of life turns into night

And your final breath breaks free
Tell me how it felt all alone in the castle
Painting a mask of cheer over misery
Knowing you caused your solitude directly

{ 5 }

I repeatedly lost myself in him
  This stranger who I was convinced I knew
With his lies, he always pulled me back in

My blind faith in him gave him confidence
With each deceit,my distrust in him grew
I lost sight of me when I was with him

He always knew I would come back to him
Apologizing, never needing to
By telling lies, he would pull me back in

Loving him equates to being a sin
They were just words to him, the "I love you"s
I consistently lost myself in him

For a while, I never thought it would end
The inescapable force just like glue
With his lies, he pulled me back in

But eventually I did leave him
I summoned the strength to bid him adieu
I repeatedly lost myself in him
He pulled me in until I was a stranger, too

Putting your all into people is very tiresome
It always leaves you empty afterwards
When the inevitable end comes

{ 7 }

L eft
   Pain
Right
Pain
No matter what route I choose to take
I'm always the one to blame

Right
Pain
Left
Pain
I watch every move that I make
There's shattered glass all over the place

I'm counting the seconds
Tracing my steps
Counting my blessings
Holding my breath

Left
Pain
Right
Pain
Whether the anger is real or it's fake
I'm always the one to blame

{ **8** }

Wandering through a field of green
But memories haunt me
Memories of not being heard
Memories of not being seen

Walking through a field of green
And yet I keep stopping
There are obstacles ahead of me
There are monsters that are lurking

Traveling through a field of green
But everything goes dark
I am in my mind, the monsters in my head
This is what I feel inside my heart

Wandering through a field of green
Yet the green has now turned brown
Wondering how to change it back
Yet I know the answer now

You took things too far
    You played with my heart
Now it's broken and scarred

I'm trapped
    in a never ending
cycle

{ 11 }

You always hear the stories of happily ever after
    But what about the ones ending in disaster?

You always hear the stories of getting to "I do"
But what about the ones that are over all too soon?

I had love
I lost it

I harbored hate
Still feel it

And I still have the feeling
That you made a mistake in leaving

I had bliss
I lost it

I felt pain
Still got it

But I'd still take you back
If I'm being honest

They say when it rains, it pours
 Well, I don't want to be in the storm anymore

The droplets are hammering down
My pain is now a deafening sound

The water has soaked through my clothes
The coldness has entered my bones

They say this too shall pass
But never how long it will last

They say when it rains, it pours
Well, I can't take being in the storm much more

I try so hard
Do all the little things
But they never seem to matter to you
In the way that they matter to me

{ **14** }

I hear you're going around saying "love for free"
    That's bold of you
Because you never loved me

And I miss a year ago
When I believed that you did
It was much easier for you than for me to forget
Times were simpler back then

Take my spirit
     Take my soul
Take my heart
I'm yours to hold

Take my anger
Take my pain
Take my sadness
When only memories of you remain

H atred is just an extension of love
Hate is love that has been hurt

{ 17 }

The sun shines through the trees
    Peeking through the leaves

Its rays hit me
Bathing me in heat

I smile at the memories
The nostalgia, it's sweet

I bask in the hot beams
Finally feeling free

{ **18** }

Taking the pain day-by-day
    Waiting for it all to fade
Silver linings - why do they sometimes look more like grey?
Waiting for the rain to wash the pain away

{ 19 }

R ed flags through rose-colored glasses just look like flags
Once they're off, you see what you really have

{ 19 }

{ **20** }

Little moments of happiness
    Found even in the darkest of nights
Little pieces of heaven
Falling down to make you smile
Don't let these moments pass you by

Smiling at strangers on subways
Blowing out the candles on your cake on your birthday
Even in your deepest heartache
These moments can help take the pain away
Don't let these moments pass you by

Whether it's everyday bygones
That you now take for granted
Or rare occasions
In which happiness is planted
Don't let these moments pass you by

Little moments of happiness
No matter how they appear
Little pieces of heaven
Signaling healing is near
Don't let these moments pass you by

If perfection was a person
I swear she would be you

{ 22 }

Sometimes I sleep at noon
    Just to escape the pain of losing you
Curtains drawn, lights off
I'm all alone in a pitch-black room
Fighting to escape you

The sadness comes in like a raging storm
A wave of black and grey
Crashing over me, rain after a sunny day

The pain hurts, but sometimes I want more
I don't push the feelings away
I don't keep the memories at bay
But other times, I need to escape

I'll be smiling one second, then crying just as fast
Like happiness is a stranger, simply waving as he rushes past
And when the drizzle of losing you becomes a monsoon
Sometimes I sleep at noon

{ 23 }

Words like knives
    Each one digging the blade in a little deeper
Touch like ice
There's distance despite you pulling me closer

Unfocused eyes
Looking in my direction but slightly over my shoulder
The close of a fight
Yet I still haven't gotten any closure

We've been dancing this dance for months now
Just going through the motions
It's been slowly ripping my heart out
Because it's an indicator for the ending

I try as hard as I can
I'll fight for as long as I must
But the feeling of losing you is sinking in
And pretty soon it'll be goodbye for us

{ **24** }

For the longest time, all I saw was grey
     Dark nights followed by rainy days
But then you came my way

Suddenly, I was swimming in a sea of hues
Only the brightest colors, no dreary blues
All due to the thought of you

Red, yellow, purple, green
So many colors washing over me
Nothing able to dull their vibrancy

Orange, indigo, teal, pink
You've got my heart rethinking "no vacancy"
Nothing compares to when you're next to me

For the longest time, all I saw was grey
Feeling big lows as I chased small highs
I thought nothing could take the pain away
But now Cloud Nine feels right in sight

{ **25** }

I wasn't looking for love
    I was in a really tough spot
  You took my battered trust and built it back up

  I wasn't looking for love
  But I'll give it all that I've got
  As long as you promise to be careful with my heart

  Because darling, I was a mess before I met you
  And darling, now I'd be a mess without you

{ 26 }

S he is love
    The way her eyes shine bright, conveying every emotion she is feeling
    Betraying every secret she is hiding

She is trust
The way she's clear; she hates lying
All she ever gives is honesty

She is happiness
The way her smile lights up the room
Her infectious laughter taking over you

She is light
The way her presence is always felt
You crave to have her around

She is love
The way she supports without judgment
Only steps in when you need it

She is her
Can't bear to be without her
Not a thing I would change about her

{ 27 }

You're gone
        And I'm left here, not sure what to do
I will never again see the girl I once knew
And I don't know what to do

You're gone
And it still feels so surreal
But I suppose you were gone for a long time
The girl in my arms no longer mine

You were gone before I realized it
Everything happened so fast
We fell in love in the blink of an eye
And just as quickly, we left it all in the past

Forever turned into never
"You're mine" became a lie
And now you're gone
And I have to convince myself that I'm fine

{ **28** }
{ 55 }

When darkness is all you see inside
         How can you see the light?
I even expect to see darkness on the outside
As if I am going blind

{ **29** }

Yellow rays, green leaves
    Bright sunshine, it feels so sweet
Washing over me

I really, really loved her
    I loved the smiles and the laughter
But she turned into a different person
And said that was her true version
So much for my happily ever after

{ 31 }

I tell people I'm fine whenever they ask questions
   It's easier to just avoid suspicions
Why should I tell them I can't sleep at night?
Why should I admit the pain feels inescapable?
I feel like I'm drowning
Suffocating
I can't get out of this spiral

I tell people that I'm healing
That I'm getting through the days of my life
Why should I tell them I still cry at night?
Why should I admit I'd give anything to have carefree childhood
back?
Some days I feel lighter
Like I can survive these waters
But others all I see is black

So I tell people I'm fine
It's easier to do
But it cuts like a knife
I feel like I'm dying inside

$$\{\ 32\ \}$$

You're like gravity
Something about you keeps pulling me back in
Even though I repeatedly get hurt in the end

Being pulled down
Falling
Yet I just keep going

Maybe some part of me is a masochist
Maybe I like the pain
Maybe that's why I can't stay away

Or maybe you're so deep inside my head
I keep recalling the past
Wishing we could go back to that

Whatever it is
It's like gravity
Repeatedly pulling me back in
Even though I repeatedly get hurt again and again

{ 33 }

We met by chance
We loved by choice
When the odds were stacked against us
We made it background noise

And I love when you call to say you miss me
And those nights we talk until 2am
I love listening to your breathing
Even out
As our waking hours come to an end

I never knew what love was until I met you
I never knew what I was missing out on
I feel at home when I'm around you
I feel content because I have you

$$\{\ 34\ \}$$

It's hard not having you around anymore
  It's hard not to feel your absence
It's hard not to repeatedly tell my memories of you that I will always love you

Your spot in the bed hasn't changed since you left
Your pillow still has a you-shaped indent
The only difference is when I reach out, the warmth has long since turned cold
And when I speak your name, I am met with silence
Reminding me that I am now alone

I've stopped being home as much
It's easier to be out, to pretend you'll still be waiting to greet me when I return
For years you were my constant
I never knew I could feel this much hurt

I didn't think the last time I saw you would be the last
But you left this world almost overnight
You left it all in the past
So now this poem is my final goodbye

{ 35 }

I romanticize romance
     But it's nothing like the movies
  There's no almost-breakup that ends in grand gestures to get back together
  Or climbing fire escapes to profess one's love, all the while holding flowers

I romanticize romance
But it's nothing like the novels
I've never had someone prove they're never leaving
I've never had someone truly fight for me

I hear the words
And they're all the same
But the actions are where it's lacking
I need the little things to fall back on
Not just whispers that make it easy for backtracking

I romanticize romance
But it never works out well for me
I've always given my everything
But they never give their all to me

{ **36** }

It's not my first time here
    And it surely won't be the last
I tend to escape here when things get bad

A bustling oasis
Filled with no judgment
A rushing city
That's perfect to get lost in

I listen to the traffic
As I drift off to sleep
What some people consider chaotic
I let give me peace
To you it might be a nuisance
To me it's a sweet melody

Someday my presence may be permanent
Someday my "visit" may turn to "live in"
But for now I escape here when things get bad
I let the Big Apple offer up all the happiness that it has

{ 37 }

I have so many thoughts running through my head
     And I just can't catch a break
Tell me it's going to be okay
Even if it's fake

I grip this pen tighter
As my hand begins to shake
I can see everything we built going down in flames
But I just can't pull away

They say nothing perfect lasts forever
But I thought you'd be my saving grace
So lie, tell me everything will be okay
Even when I'm the one to blame

Pull me closer and closer
Hold me as if I'm about to break
Don't let go or the pieces might fade away
And for that, I don't have the strength

After everything we've been through
I can't watch you walk away
I can't hear the words you're about to say
Knowing I could've been the change

If letting go means losing grip
That's not a step I'm ready to take

So tell me lies, say it'll be okay
Even if it's fake

So tell me lies, say it'll be okay
Even if it's fake

{ 38 }

Let me love you
    When you can't love yourself

When your troubles are weighing on your shoulders
When the weight of the world is dragging you under
Put it all on me
Let me love you

When the light at the end of the tunnel is hard to see
When the rain is hiding the silver lining
Turn to me
Let me love you

When nothing is going right
And there is no end to the struggles in sight
I'll do my best to make you happy
Let me love you

When you look in the mirror and only see flaws
I will be quick to discount them all
Believe me
Let me love you

Let me love you
When you can't love yourself

{ 39 }

Her eyes are darker now
    They've lost their shine
They used to be clear and bright

A cerulean blue turned almost navy now
Tarnished
Almost as if they've lost their light

It makes sense if you ask me
Even though it's a dreary sight
Happiness no longer shines through her eyes

They used to be radiant
Lit up like a summer sky
But now they're as dark as night

{ **40** }

S he calms me

When my mind is a raging ocean
Each thought like a wave crashing over the next
She speaks, her words like medicine
She calms me

When my blood feels like lava coursing through my veins
When my skin feels aflame
She holds me, her touch soothing the pain
She calms me

When my stomach is doing somersaults
And everything feels like it's all my fault
She simply looks my way, her eyes conveying everything she desires to say
She calms me

When everything is going wrong and there is nothing left to say
I know I can count on her at the end of every day
And even when I really am the one to blame
She loves me, reminding me that with black and white there also comes grey
And with that love
She calms me

{ **41** }

I tell people you passed away
   It's the easier thing to say

In truth, I'm not completely wrong
Your body is here, but the girl I knew is long gone

It saves me from the pitying glances
It keeps people from asking if I will give you more chances

I gave you enough
Each betrayal chipping away at my trust

So I repeat my well-rehearsed speech
I tell people you're dead when you're really just dead to me

{ 42 }

You hugged me
I hugged you back but
We didn't fit together like we used to
We weren't what we were used to

Our love was founded on the thrill
Sometimes I stop to wonder, was it even real?
Did we love us?
Or just the thought of us?

Loving you was like stepping out of the shower
Refreshing, and yet
You can't see the full picture
There's fog on the mirror

A dewy substance layered in a fine mist
Hiding it
A hazy image
The film hard to miss

Was I what you imagined I would be?
Or was I better left as a fantasy?
Some far-off person, hard to reach
A goal left unachieved

Maybe you should have left me at a thought
The idea being incomparable

When unattainable, I'm desirable
But when attained, it's less than magical

You let go, stepped back
I did the same but
You took my emotions with you
All I'm left with is painful residue

{ **43** }

I trusted you without borders
    There was no limit to my love
    Maybe that was my mistake
    Maybe this pain was the price to pay

{ **44** }

Eternally
    She was eternally mine
Until just like that, she was gone
As if her existence was no more than a whisper of the wind
Whistling through the trees
Before I could blink
Her presence in my life disappeared
As if she didn't know what she meant to me
As if she didn't know that my heart would sink
And that her leaving would cut, deep
And that I would bleed
Eternally

Sadness
    Emotional vastness
Smile
You're fine

Heart aching
Chest hurting
Smile
You're fine

Eyes stinging
Tears burning
Smile
You're fine

Throat closing
Breath escaping
Smile
You're fine

$$\{ \ 46 \ \}$$

Your eyes bore into mine
    No, bore isn't the right word
This is anything but boring

Your eyes gaze into mine
Do I know you from somewhere?
Have I met you in another life?

An unwavering stare, almost familiar
My heart leaping at the exposure
My brain searching for answers

Maybe you meant a lot to me in the past
Too far back for me to remember
My soul transporting me back

Your eyes melt into mine
I feel like I know you
Like we are connected

Your eyes leave mine
As you walk away, my spirit goes with you
As if it knows what love is

{ 47 }

Always and forever
    Didn't last that long
Ten months
One day
And our song had been sung

I knew from the first look, I was a goner
    Could have had anyone you wanted
Why me?

Love is a cruel mistress
　　She yearns to put on a show
And revels in making you fall alone

{ **50** }

Tell me how long it's going to feel like this
    If this is love, I don't want to know what love is

I spent countless nights
With you by my side
Thought you would never leave

You acted like everything was fine
Then you took me by surprise
I just wish you were back here with me

Now when I look in the mirror
I don't know the person I see
I don't recognize the unhappy
And I'm missing half of me

{ **50** }

$$\{\ 51\ \}$$

It's inescapable when it's carried inside of you
  A stormcloud you can't get away from
A burgeoning abyss
Unraveling
Coming undone

Sometimes the pain felt deepest
Is the kind that can't be seen
It's held buried deep down
Loathed but never ignored
The dark, cataclysmal storm

Often there's no exact reason
Just a general sense of despair
So you push it down
Try to block it out
And pretend that it isn't there

But it's inescapable when it's carried inside of you
A shadow never far behind
A black figure watching
Following
Never too far from your mind

{ **52** }

One year ago today, you were a stranger
　　We had never met, only crossed paths in the most ironic of
ways
　　I dreamed of a love like the one we had
　　Of always having a hand to hold
　　A love that's all-consuming
　　Epic

　　But today you are still a stranger
　　I never knew the real you, not even to this day
　　I have nightmares about the love we had
　　About the lies you told
　　A love that was terrifying
　　Tragic

{ **53** }

I always told you that you were the girl of my dreams
You're still haunting them

{ 53 }

{ **54** }

Watching someone you love lose themselves is almost as painful
as losing yourself
Or maybe it's more painful, in a way
Because when you lose yourself, you know no one else is to blame

It's different when it's somebody else
It's harder to watch and not be able to help
It's painful to wait for them to save theirself

{ 54 }

{ **55** }

Your eyes
    They're so easy to get lost in
Deep hazel, a mix of brown and green
Mesmerizing when the light hits

They say the eyes are the windows to the soul
The sun shines bright through yours
Warmth falling over me
Someone worth fighting for

{ 56 }

Fighting
  For a spot
Everywhere

Fighting
For a breath
Running out of air

Struggling
To stand out
Maybe I should blend in

Camouflage
Guard my heart
Let nobody in

{ 57 }

Yellow was all I saw for months
        Or maybe it was gold
Licking at the edges of my vision
With such precision
Lighting things up so much that I never wanted to lose its hold

But one betrayal at a time
That illumination started to flicker
As my trust broke
With every lie that you spoke
My love for you began to wither

As if someone turned out the lights in a room
The colors got darker
The gold faded
And faded
As if someone was slowly sliding down a dimmer

The rose-colored glasses soon turned red
That was all I saw in my anger
When I realized that I barely knew you
I also learned that pink wasn't the right hue
Red was the color

It reminds me of a storm
    Raging inside of me

It starts out small
A drizzle of rain here
A gust of wind there
A growing rage in the form of displeasure

Then the feelings get stronger
Lapping at my chest
Little waves on the shore

With each hostile word said
With each inconvenience met
They grow a little bigger

A flurry of words in the form of insults
A shoulder as cold as ice
Anger overtakes me like a tidal wave
Before lashing out, I barely think twice

When all is said and done
There is nothing left but calm
As if the hurricane that came through
Broke down all my walls

{ 59 }

I nside me there's a storm
   Wind raging
Windows breaking

It's tearing at my heart
Lights flickering
Walls shaking

I'm being torn apart
It's what my feelings do
When there's no you

{ **60** }

Maybe I fight to feel something
    Anger in the moment
Fear of your response
Relief when it's over

Maybe I fight to see if you care
If you didn't, it wouldn't get to you
You wouldn't react
You wouldn't snap back

Maybe I fight for the reassurance
That making up always brings
The reassurance that I'm worth it
That you'll always fight for me

$$\{ \ 61 \ \}$$

It's funny how it ended
  Slowly, then all at once
Kind of like a storm but
I knew there was nowhere to go but up

But I thought we were on the right side of rock bottom
I thought we were on the same page to keep trying
So I put all my effort into you
As you put in just enough to get through

And looking back
I see it clearly
Thinking back
You always knew just what to say
For things to be okay
But they didn't turn out that way

And looking back
I should've been smarter
Thinking back
I missed the signs
Told myself it'll be alright
I didn't read between the lines

{ **62** }

I grieved through anger
      Breaking things left and right
   So my surroundings would match my broken heart

   You didn't leave any part of me whole when you left
   Not a single piece of me was spared
   Maybe it was always meant to work out like that

   Maybe my heart stopping when we first met was because it antic-
ipated breaking
   Maybe my breath left me because it knew it would be taken by
pain anyway
   Maybe my body was preparing me for my entire being's shatter-
ing

   Maybe
   Just maybe
   All along it knew
   Maybe it was preparing me for you

The sun beats down on me
        I close my eyes
Feeling my worries and cares evaporate
Like they are droplets of water in the unwavering heat

I hear children laughing in the distance
Dogs barking
Announcing their presence
In this moment, I have no fears

I know it won't last
It never does
All of my problems will soon come back

But in this moment
This blissful moment
All I need is to be right here

{ **64** }

Maybe it was the sparkle in your eyes
Or the way you always left me tongue-tied

Maybe it was your loving attention
Or your unwavering devotion
That made me feel so lucky to call you mine

I felt like I was it for you
The one
A perfectly balanced two
Like I was the moon and you were the sun

We were so perfectly written
But like our symbols, we were among the stars
Things fell out of place
And we damaged our hearts

Or maybe it was always meant to work out this way
With me being just another chapter in your book
Maybe I was the fool who, in the end, got played
And maybe I'm stupid for craving another try at what history
took

{ 65 }

Nighttime used to be my favorite time
        Darkness enveloping me
Silence being broken by the sound of your breathing

I loved knowing you were here with me
That I was yours and you were mine
That the future was ours to find

But now the darkness in my chest
Is no longer filled with light
Now the hardest time is the night
Because the silence is always eerily quiet
With only my thoughts present to break it

{ **66** }

It was a fire inside my mind
My thoughts burning me alive

These feelings are fighting inside me
    I feel like I'm going down
There's not much fight left in me
I'll surrender without a sound

I want to be mad
I don't want to care
But the only feeling I'm feeling is scared

I want to scream
I want to shout
About how much I hate myself right now

{ **68** }

As the world spins in circles
    It is hard to stay awake
And as I watch the clock tick forward
I lose another day

I want you here with me
As much as I want to breathe
Why did you have to go?
Why did you have to leave?

Sinking
As my world turns upside down
I'd surrender
If I could make a sound

{ 68 }

From the day we met
We were too close
Always way too close

It didn't give us space to breathe
It didn't give us room to grow
And slowly we began to choke

$$\{\ 70\ \}$$

Who could've predicted I'd grow to love brown more than blonde?
I've always been one to give in to darkness
Who would have thought I'd learn to appreciate hazel more than blue?
I've always been a sucker for variance
Spontaneity, adventures
Never wanting to get stuck in the same old patterns
Maybe that's why it didn't work out well with you
Maybe that's why I chose hazel over blue

{ 71 }

Karma is after me
 After all, she took you away

Everything has turned to just a memory
One that's slowly beginning to fade

Even when I try to hold on
To everything we ever made

Fate is still laughing at me
My dreams showing me what I crave

Yearning fills my body, my soul
And yet I know I'm the one to blame

{ **72** }

Maybe you were the right person at the wrong time
      The stars didn't stay aligned
Maybe you were who I'm meant to be with
It's the only thing that seems right

Maybe I'm made for you
And maybe you're made for me
Maybe this love is true
And not just a fantasy

Maybe you were the right person at the wrong time
You took over my frame of mind
Maybe I'm who you're meant to be with
Only later on in life

It's easier to think of you as imaginary
    Some sort of a fever dream
Because then I don't have to face
That I lost the best of me

Your smile was just the sunshine
The radiant sparkle being mistaken for teeth
Your laugh was just some windchimes
The sound floating along on the breeze

Your hugs were simply my blanket
Wrapped tightly around me at night
My cats came to yank it off
The cold being mistaken for you leaving me behind

So after everything is said and done
And I'll never see you again
It's easier to pretend you were never real to begin with
Than it is to accept losing my partner, my best friend

{ 74 }

Monday I get home
  Dinner is ready
You met me in the kitchen
Arms wrap around me

Tuesday I wake up
With a kiss on the cheek
A warm arm over my waist
Happy birthday to me

Wednesday is much the same
Our anniversary
And even in your work breaks
You shower kisses onto me

How can you treat someone like that
When you know you're going to leave
My heart is not a game
That you can play until you beat

You acted like everything was okay
You were falling more in love everyday
Then unexpectedly left me with no warning
It still feels like a very bad dream

75

An ocean between us
      Even though we're side-by-side
Can't shake this feeling
Something will go wrong tonight

And if you say we're all good
Then I'll know you lied
Because how can you keep pulling away
If everything is fine

All I want is to move forward
But you'd rather leave me behind
I knew something would go wrong tonight
I guess all along I was right

Maybe it's all my fault
Maybe I'll never be enough
Maybe empty rooms and broken hearts
Are all I conjure up

Maybe you were the right person
At the wrong time

Maybe we went too fast
To read the signs

Maybe we're still living it up
In a different life

Maybe we're still so happy
Just letting everything else pass us by

What would have happened if we met a little later in life?
What would have happened if we actually got our timing right?
Would we still be here, residue from the fallout?
3am, hoping you'll call now?

Maybe you were the right person
At the wrong time
Maybe we're still living it up
In a different life

78

It's okay if you don't like me
    I don't like me, either
Too passionate, too sensitive
Too curious, inquisitive
Too much to handle at any given moment
I'll likely lead you to an explosion
I find your buttons and I push
And I push
A n d I p u s h...

After all, words are only words
    Until they hurt too bad
And time is only time
Until it goes too fast

{ **80** }

E ffortless
    Loving you is effortless

Your gentle embrace like the caress of the breeze
Your comforting eyes as green as the trees
Your melodic laugh as sweet as could be
Your presence is calming; you're home to me

And even if we were separated by oceans and seas
Mountains and hilltops as far as the eye could see
I would still keep on loving you, effortlessly
And keep waiting on the day that you would come home to me

{ **81** }

People keep saying it'll get better
    Then why is it only getting worse?
I haven't spent any time being bitter
Because I know that I hurt you first

Going back, I would do things differently
I would think before I act
The consequences hit me drastically
I wish I could change the past

Losing you felt like losing a part of me
And I'd do anything to get it back
Because all along, you were my Princess Charming
I guess that's why I fell for you so fast

So people keep saying it'll get better
But I highly doubt that it will

As everyday my hope goes more and more downhill

$$\{\ 82\ \}$$

W ish I had known our time wasn't well-spent
I'm starting to see our goodbye as heaven-sent

$$\{\ 82\ \}$$

{ **83** }

You've imprinted yourself on my mind
Like a tattoo that will never fade

{ **84** }

Lost a lot of weight because I wasn't eating right
Lost a lot of sleep because the hardest time's at night
Tried to focus on myself but you stayed on my mind

Lost a lot of motivation to carry on
With you gone
My mind's on repeat
Saying please come back to me

I keep thinking back to kissing in parking lots
Playing she loves me, loves me not
Sending novel-length messages
How could I forget?

And I know I'll never find a love like this again
But I know that you think that we're better off as friends
And I also know that I'm the cause of it

If any pair was perfect it would be me and you
If anything was worth it, it'd be fighting hard for you

The first night that I met you
I knew that you were the one
I drove an hour after midnight
Just to be with you when I saw the sun

You were my new addiction

I'm always happiest in your presence
But that's the thing about addictions
Often someday they get broken

Maybe I shouldn't be texting my ex
But we all make mistakes
In heartbreak

And maybe I shouldn't be replying to you
After what you put me through
Yet I wait

And maybe I'm still a little lost
Dealing with a tragic, shattered heart
But my only hope
Is to learn how to cope

{ **86** }

When we met, I had my guard up
    My heart had been broken and scarred
But you let yourself right in
I loved you from the start

So I ruined another night
    I started another fight
I don't know why you're still here
Looking so sincere
Saying all the things you know I like to hear

{ **88** }

I don't want to be that ex you don't want to talk about
    Because you say one thing and it all starts rushing out
  It's funny how things were so good then they went so south

  I don't ever want to be your half-past-two drunk call on Friday
night
  Talk for hours just catching up on life
  Until you disappear the moment we see the light

  Way down the line
  I hope you're still mine

{ 89 }

I often say the wrong thing at the wrong time
    Get so caught up in the joke that I miss the punchline
I've been trying to learn my wrong from right
But I heard these things take time

{ 89 }

{ **90** }

I'm sitting here in silence
    But it's never been so loud
My head screams, "Are you leaving?"
My heart doesn't make a sound

{ 91 }

I'm just a little in my head but that's the usual
    Feel three words on my lips, told myself I'd never say love
Been burned before but I'm learning that's not us

And if I don't tell you that your smile lights up the room
Just know that I'm thinking it
And if I don't tell you that your eyes rival the moon
Just know that I'm thinking that, too

Because you are everything perfect to me
And you're the only one that I see
So if I don't tell you that I love you
Just know I'm getting close to that, too

{ 92 }

Are we not all the same at the end of the day?
Our worlds drifting away
To a faraway place

{ 93 }

{ 185 }

The thing about it being almost love is that it wasn't love
    And the thing about it being drawn out too long is that it
almost ruined us

{ 94 }

I stand in the bathroom, the tile cold beneath my feet
    The mirror stares back at me
My eyes hone in on an image unlike the one that others see
The scene is crippling

{ 95 }

You say you miss me
        I miss you, too
Of course I do

But I don't miss the lying and the fighting
Always holding my breath
The sneaking and the cheating
Always coming second-best

Now that you're gone, my life is a mess
But with your love, darling, you put me to the test

I have a habit of making excuses for others
But there's no more I can make for you
You dug your own grave, made your own bed
Honey, this is on you

{ **96** }

G rief isn't linear
      You can't simply close the door
To you, I no longer matter
But I will always be a little bit yours

{ 97 }

I know that what fate gives
    It can just as easily take away
    Nothing is set in stone
    Nothing truly stays the same

{ 98 }

My heart still longs for you
    Even after all this time
The pain, it never truly goes away
It just becomes normal, a part of each day

Thoughts of you plague me
I fear there's no escaping
I ponder over what would happen
If you passed me on the street

Would you recognize me?
Would you say hi to me?
Would you keep on walking
Looking away the second our eyes meet?

If you did, I would deserve it
My fears led to a suffocating hold
And if you're happier now, you deserve it
Our chapter can end, our story told

I guess what they say is true
The punishment fits the crime
I broke your heart, my grip too tight
And now I dream of a love that will never again be mine

{ 99 }

I've been up all night thinking
    Just some nighttime daydreaming

Be careful with what is said

Be careful with what is said
    You never know how long it will replay in someone's head
Or what will push them over the edge